DEDICATION

To my ancestors: Black, White and Native

To my daughters: Khadijah, A'ishah and Zainab

To my grandsons: Solomon, Amir and Talib

Creating a world that works for all of them…

IN MEMORY

For my mother: Ernestine Moore Sanders, again

Previous Books by Sharif Abdullah

Abdullah, Sharif. *The Power of One: Authentic Leadership in Turbulent Times*. Commonway Institute (1st Edition), 1990; New Society Publishers (2nd Edition), 1995; (3rd Edition), 2007.

Abdullah, Sharif. *Creating a World That Works for All*. Berrett-Kohler Publishers, 1999.

Abdullah, Sharif. *The Soul of a Terrorist: Reflections on Our War with "The Other"*. Chapter Seven in *The Psychology of Terrorism (Volume I of four volumes)*. Greenwood Press, 2002.

Abdullah, Sharif. *Finding Our Way in the Land of the Blind – Essays on Terrorism and Steps for Living in a Violence-Free World*. Commonway Institute, 2003.

Abdullah, Sharif. *Sips from the River of Wisdom*. Commonway Institute, 2004.

Abdullah, Sharif. *Searching for Depth*. Commonway Institute, 2004.

Abdullah, Sharif (with Dr. Donna Beegle). *The Class Continuum*. Communication Across Barriers, 2006.

Table of Contents

Acknowledgments

Where did the thoughts contained in this book originate?

There are a number of energies and influences that conspired to create this book. No idea springs from a vacuum. Every concept is born from some antecedent. In Buddhism, this is called "dependent arising".

Some influences are easy to track; some more subtle. My primary influences include…

Acknowledging The Divine…

The Divine rains upon all – but only some of us get wet. For many of us, we don't WANT to acknowledge any Transcendental Reality. Or, we are taught by our religion that only the guys in the robes are qualified to talk to/for/with The Divine. Or, we don't make the connection with The Divine because we are afraid of what we might hear.

My spiritual practice consists of paying attention to the gentle voice… and being silent enough within to listen.

All energy arises from The Divine, by whatever name. This book is the result of processes that can be traced back to the Big Bang… and Before. For that, I am thankful.

Acknowledging Sarvodaya…

Many people know of my 15 year involvement with the Sarvodaya Shramadana organization in Sri Lanka. But, most don't know how it started.

I first met the legendary Dr. A. T. Ariyaratne ("Ari" to his Western friends) in a book, "In the Footsteps of Gandhi" by Catherine Ingram. Something struck me about an organization that did not focus on the "pieces" of development, but looked at the totality of the person and the totality of the society, the "awakening of all".

Later, I had the opportunity to meet Ari in 1995 when he came to the US to accept an award. At that time, he invited me to Sri Lanka. Six months later, I was there. During my first trip to Sri Lanka, Ari put me to work... and I've been working ever since.

As an advisor to Sarvodaya, I have been involved with how to best implement Sarvodaya's outstanding and comprehensive philosophy. It is a true JOY to work with an organization where the vision, focus, direction and ethics of the organization are clear, coherent and consistent.

Along with working with Ari, I have had the opportunity to work with all of the members of his large family, especially his daughter Dr. Charika Marasinghe and his grandson Janantha.

And, most significantly, I have worked closely with his eldest son, Dr. Vinya Ariyaratne, the Executive Director of Sarvodaya. For the past decade, my close friendship and ongoing working relationship with Vinya has been a mainstay of my life. I have come to respect his vision (different from yet compatible with his father's), his genius at strategic planning, his commitment to the concept of peace and his commitment to encourage Sarvodaya in becoming the inter-religious and multi-ethnic organization it aspires to be.

Through 15 years of meditating, planning, strategizing, implementing, arguing, evaluating, laughing, visioning, more arguing and celebrating, it is impossible for me to tell where "my" ideas stop and "their" ideas start. I learned a lot. I taught a lot. We developed a lot together. Ultimately, there is no "mine" and "theirs".

It's safe to say that virtually everything in this book, cover to cover, has been influenced, directly or indirectly, through my association with Sarvodaya. If you went through this text and took out the word "relational" and replaced it with the word

"Sarvodaya", you wouldn't be far off.

This book expands, updates and even goes beyond some Sarvodaya concepts; my intention is to expand the audience for these principles. There is a global need for conscious awakening; therefore, expanding beyond the island of Sri Lanka is a must.

Acknowledging Christopher Alexander and "The Quality Without a Name"...

Another major influence for me is the work of someone I've never met in the flesh: Christopher Alexander, master architect. His book, "The Timeless Way of Building" should be read by every human being on the planet. His most important concept is "the quality without a name", something that is close to (but not the same as) concepts like, "life", "freedom", "love", "order", "wholeness", "simplicity", "eternal"... When we infuse our buildings (and our lives) with this nameless quality, we feel good about being alive. With it, we live our lives free of inner contradictions. When we ignore it, our buildings (and our lives) become ugly, dysfunctional, useless.

How you build your buildings (and how you live your life) is determined by your language. He calls the patterns that build up over time a "pattern language". Here, I call the same thing an "operating system". As I try to approximate that quality here in these pages, I acknowledge Christopher Alexander as my teacher in this regard.

Acknowledging Thomas Jefferson...

Jefferson remains an iconic hero to many – including me.

Thomas Jefferson's later work is of particular value to this book. In his later life, Jefferson was deeply unsatisfied with the role and direction of the federal government after the drafting of the Constitution. He thought that federal government had gotten too big and too powerful. (Imagine how he would feel if he saw our present bloated confusion we refer to as "government".)

Prior to his death, he advocated something he called "ward republics" – a concept I revive here in this book. It matches Mahatma Gandhi's concept of "grama swaraj" – village republics. Both Jefferson and Gandhi start from the premise that the center of government must be at the local level. Each community, each village, each ward must be independent and sovereign. You will see this concept revisited in the section on "relational power".

Acknowledging Support for this Book:

I listen to my intuition, the Inner Voice that has guided me on this incredible path that I've been taking on this planet. When that Voice said to write this book, and to have it PUBLISHED by mid-July (four months), it was the first time in decades I wanted a second opinion! I said, "Okay, I can get it done by mid-July… but, which year?"

The second thing that came through, strong and clear, was that I had to write the book alone. Over the years, I have talked with a number of friends and co-conspirators about collaborating on a book. But, my Guidance was clear: I had to "own" this writing, and be fully responsible for whatever happens next.

However, no being is an island. During the course of this writing, a number of people came forward to share my steep path. While I could have written and published this without them, I am so grateful that I did not have to! The final outcome is so much better for their assistance.

Producers:
To write a book on such a short timeline, a lot had to come together. One aspect was money. From keeping the lights on

(and the computers running!), to buying the (recycled) paper for umpteen draft manuscripts, to rolling out the information so that others learn about this book... it all gets facilitated by money.

I want to thank the people who stepped forward in response to my request for funding, including: Dianne and Chuck Adams, Lois Bell, Leslie Hamilton, Dorothy Lamb, Simone Lorenz and Bruce Cohen, Sergio Lub, Bobby Romanski and Sharon Williams. (And, my apologies if I inadvertently left someone off of the list.)

I also want to acknowledge all those who could not give money, but gave their prayers, meditations and energetic support to this effort: those prayers and energies are welcome and felt – by me and throughout our society.

Creative and Technical Contributors:

There are a lot of background activities that lie just beneath the surface of this book. It's quite a production! Writing, editing (concept edit, copy edit and line edit), typesetting, page layout, cover design and development, graphics, proof reading, research...

I want to thank the people who volunteered to provide creative and technical support and feedback, including: Don Berg, Malva Huson Brown (at 93, our most "senior" editor), Bruce Cohen, Peter and Trudy Johnson-Lenz, Miki Kashtan, Simone Lorenz, Juanita Ruth One, Bobby Romanski and Starr Sheppard-Decker.

I want to give special thanks to Bobby Romanski, who provided both financial support and TONS of technical support. The arrangement and layout of this book is largely due to him.

A GLOSSARY OF TERMS

In this book, I introduce a number of terms. Those of you familiar with "Creating a World That Works for All" will recognize terms like Keeper, Breaker and Mender. I also introduce some new terms, and give some expanded meanings for existing terms.

In a society, we communicate with words. Society is built on words. Just as we cannot build a house with defective or missing tools, we cannot build a society with words that constrain us instead of fueling our vision. It is not enough to hold a vision; we must be able to communicate it to others.

Adversarial: That which is about conflicting, opposing, or antagonistic parties or interests. The opposite of "relational".

Agent: A person who, while working independently, operates on behalf of someone or something else.

Biocidal: Relating to an agent that is destructive to living organisms.

Biophilic: Relating to an agent that is loving and appreciative to living organisms.

Breakers/Breaker Consciousness: People whose fundamental operating belief is "I am separate," and whose operating assumption is "There is not enough." The Breaker story is "Creating a World That Works for Me." Breakers treat the Earth as their own property, a life support system for them to use as they please. People operating with Breaker consciousness seek ever greater control over all aspects of life on Earth, while behaving as though they were exempt from the laws of Nature. Anyone, at any time, can act like a Breaker. And, anyone, at any time, can cease behaving like a Breaker.

Corebook: A condensation or summary of a larger work.

Culture: The set of behaviors shared by a group of people. Culture is the external indicator of a shared consciousness.

Exclusivity: Any set of behaviors based on the belief that our lives are separate, that what I do to others has no effect on me, and that all beings exist primarily to be used and controlled for my benefit.

Inclusivity: Any set of behaviors based on the awareness that our lives are inextricably linked with each other, so that whatever I do has an effect on you. Inclusivity is the Golden Rule in practice.

Keepers/Keeper Consciousness: Indigenous people who live their lives inextricably connected to their local ecology. Their fundamental operating belief is "We are One." Keepers behave as though they are a part of the Earth. For them, no one group or species is more important than any other.

Menders/Mender Consciousness: People whose fundamental operating belief is "We are One," and whose operating assumption is "There is enough for all." Menders seek to restore balance with the Earth, and consciously live their lives as an integral part of a living, sacred planet. Menders seek ways to bring healing to all beings and to the Earth.

The Mess: The nightmarish complex of societal and personal challenges and crises that afflict today's world. The Mess is incapable of being resolved with our current techniques of problem solving. The Mess is the polar opposite of the Web of Life.

Operating System: The multiple and interlocking beliefs, behaviors and processes by which people live their lives in society.

Relational: That which is about relationships (between people, other beings, the environment and the Transcendent). The opposite of "adversarial".

Spirit: The Essence, Power, Creative Intelligence, Source of Life and Transcendence that lies behind all things and is beyond human rationality and control. Awareness of Spirit may arise both inside and outside the context of "religion."

Spiritual starvation: A condition in which inner contact with Spirit and its many expressions is blocked.

Volition: The faculty or power of using one's will; the capability of conscious choice, decision and intention.

Web of Life: The totality of life on Earth, seen in all its interconnectedness. The Web is a self-regulating, self-evolving system of interlocking organisms, species and subsystems.

If we cultivate integrity, generosity, compassion, and relationships...

... the way we cultivate the love of money and the suspicion of each other...

We will live in a profoundly different world.

Our next 100 years will be intensely spiritual – but unlike anything currently espoused by religious institutions.

INTRODUCTION

This is a book of wisdom.
It is intelligence about relationships with
ourselves, with each other, with the natural
world, and with the Divine.

We need something besides sensibility and rationality. We need WISDOM.

The bad news: We, the human species, are going in the wrong direction. We are headed for destruction, unless we change our ways.

The species that destroys itself, destroys the Earth and disregards the Divine is simply not intelligent enough to continue to inhabit this planet.

We don't know what to do.

We are on this destructive course, mainly because we are not asking the right questions. Most of us aren't asking any questions at all.

The good news: some of us are evolving.

Some of us understand that the wisdom teachers were laying the foundations for a new human being, the next step of our evolutionary road. It's time for us to boldly take the step that lies before us.

Few recognize how close we are to human extinction... We will not be colonizing Mars. In the centuries to come, we can speak of success if there are still human colonies on Earth.

Albert Bates

We need a new <u>operating system</u>, a way to live in this present-day society.

We have to live in this world... not in denial and not in fantasy. We need an operating system that we can enact in our day-to-day living, yet still act in accordance with the values of the wisdom teachers and the needs of the Earth. We need to replace our violent, immoral societies with something else – a Relational Operating System.

Collectively, we will reawaken Spirit on Earth.

What this Book Does -- And Does Not -- Contain.

A "corebook" (my term) is a writing of essential thought, designed to be the essence of one or more other writings. Think "Cliffs Notes".

For example: The US government consists of legal documents that total hundreds of volumes, literally millions of pages of text. However, the <u>core</u> of the US government is the six handwritten pages of the Constitution.

I don't expect anyone to "get" the Relational Operating System from this corebook. There's not enough detail in this book. On purpose.

But, I do expect people to WANT it, to want the Relational Operating System. When they finish this book, I expect people to say, "Yes, this is great! Now, show me how it works!" I don't expect anyone to say, "After reading this corebook, I understand how this whole thing works." That's not the intention of this book.

The Germ of the Seed...

I will remind you of my "promise" at the end of this book. You are about to experience the skeleton or core of a concept, not the full concept itself. If it leaves you with a feeling of "This is great, but where's the beef (or tofu)?", know that it's coming. The full sourcebook, "Spirit on Earth", will be available "soon".

Want to know how to apply these ideas? Look around you. The seeds of the new society are lying all around you. The seeds are within you.

As highlighted by my friend Paul Hawken in his book, "Blessed Unrest", there are millions of us, all around the world, stumbling toward a fundamentally different society. We're making it up as we go along. The purpose of this book is to shine a light onto our process, to connect the dots so that we can see the underlying coherent pattern.

This book gives us an idea of the vision, a glimpse of the far shore. This vision will help us to avoid the depression that nothing can be done. It also helps us to avoid sinking into complacency – that just because we've taken Step One, we don't have to take Step Two. Until we all can say that the world works for all beings, there is always a next step.

Stay Tuned

This corebook is intended to be the first part of three interconnected writings.

"Seven Seeds for a New Society" is the skeleton, the framework of an idea: that we need a new society, built on values, visions and strategies for action and behavior: an operating system.

But, a skeleton doesn't get around without some "meat". Assuming there is support and interest, I will finish the second book, the source book, in about 6 months. My working title for this is "Spirit on Earth: An Operating System for a Spiritual Society". That book will contain much more detail, as well as stories of my experiences in various parts of the world in attempting to implement aspects of the Relational Operating System.

I also will be supporting the Relational Operating System by talks and by a workshop series on the key aspects of the system.

Courtesy to the Messenger

Before we begin, I'd like to remind you that this is a message. It's the same message that's been offered by many before me.

If the message resonates with your Heart, then give thanks to the One that originated the message – not me, but the Transcendent Divine.

If the message stirs up anger, resentment,

rage… please remember, as a matter of courtesy… don't shoot the messenger. (I invite you to closely examine what gets stirred up by these words. Yes, it may be that I'm crazy. But, it may be that there is something powerful and hidden within yourself, waiting until now to emerge for resolution.)

If you think you can do a better job of articulating a transformative society… Great! Go for it. Don't *criticize* me – *out-perform* me. If you think I didn't do it right, do something better!

Our world is in grave, grave trouble, but our world also rests in good hands, because, actually, it rests in yours.

Roger Walsh

Seven Seeds

Cut an apple with a knife, slicing it in half along its equator. What you will see in its five-point star pattern are seeds.

You are looking at potential apple trees. Everything that an apple tree needs to become a mature tree, blossoming with thousands of flowers and hundreds of apples, is awaiting the correct application of sunlight and water.

Slice into the vision of this book with your mind. What you are looking at is tens of thousands of human-scale societies. You are looking at billions of humans with enough food, water, shelter and energy to live fulfilling, empowered lives. You are looking at human ingenuity harnessed in service to other human beings and to the Earth. You are looking at Spirit being practiced not at weekend workshops, but in all ways, every day.

A Spiritual Society?

What do I mean by "spiritual society"? Am I proposing a world where everyone goes to church every Sunday? (Since I don't, that proposal would be a little hypocritical.)

A "spiritual society" is one that is motivated by the Spirit, a society based on the Dalai Lama's ideas of the Spirit:

> *"Spirituality I take to be concerned with those qualities of the human spirit -- such as love and compassion, patience, tolerance, forgiveness, contentment, a sense of responsibility, a sense of harmony -- which bring happiness to both self and others.*
>
> *"Thus spiritual practice... involves, on the one hand, acting out of concern for others' well-being. On the other, it entails transforming ourselves so that we become more readily disposed to do so. To speak of spiritual practice in any terms other than these is meaningless.*
>
> *"My call for a spiritual revolution is thus not a call for a religious revolution. Nor is it a reference to a way of life that is somehow otherworldly.... Rather, it is a call for a radical reorientation away from our habitual preoccupation with self."*

The Dalai Lama

So, a spiritual society would not necessarily have any of the trappings or rituals we associate with "religion" (although it may). A spiritual society would be motivated primarily by Transcendental values of compassion, patience, tolerance, harmony… and love.

Is it necessary to believe in The Divine in order to live a spiritual life in a spiritual society? Absolutely not. We may have radically different notions about the nature of the Divine – or even the existence of the Divine. But, that does not affect whether or not we regularly practice compassion, giving, service and love for each other, other beings and the Earth Herself.

> *"Though I do not believe that a plant will spring up where no seed has been, I have great faith in a seed. Convince me that you have a seed there, and I am prepared to expect wonders."*
>
> *Henry David Thoreau*

All we need is the correct application of our willpower.

A word about Breakers, Keepers and Menders

There are parts of this book that will resonate deep within your being. And, hopefully, there will be parts that will make you squirm or cringe.

I can identify aspects of my own behavior as "Breaker". I will bet that you can, too. That's the part of us that squirms and cringes when we bring it out for examination.

This "squirm factor" is both healthy and necessary. It means that you recognize that we're all in this together. There is no "them" to blame for the Mess that we are in. In the words of the immortal philosopher, Pogo, "We have met the enemy and he is us".

It is important for us to transcend and transform our behavior, not judge and condemn. The judging and condemning behavior (the behavior of others or your own) just leaves you stuck in the same rut. It's time to climb out of our ruts.

The opposite to the "squirm factor" is also true: there will be aspects of this book that will make you sit up a little straighter, smile a little deeper, knowing that you are on the "winning side". Knowing that, in order for "our side" to win, every being on this planet, human and otherwise, must win also.

May all beings be well;

May all beings be secure;

May all beings be happy.

Sharif Abdullah
Portland/Oregon/Cascadia/USA/Gaia
14 July 2009

Our Destiny carries us to the far shore. The near shore erodes under our feet.

The only way we'll get there is to let go of the familiar and set out across the bridge of transformation toward what we can't see...

but can envision.

SEED #1:
THE OFFERING

I offer you a window…
Who am I? Who is the person who speaks to you now, in this writing?

Some speakers on social or cultural or spiritual transformation started out as supporters of the Breaker Operating System (some unconsciously, others wholeheartedly). Subsequently, they had an "a-ha!" epiphany, then wrote a book about their change.

I never had the epiphany. I never spent much time believing that things were okay, or benefitting from the existing system. From the earliest time, I knew something was wrong.

For 50 years, since I was at least 8 years old, I have seen the necessity to change our society. I could compare the Camden, NJ version of life with the television version. I could compare what they said in the Bible to what was happening on the streets. There was quite a gap in both cases.

For over 45 years, since I was 12 years old, I have been trying to create that transformation.

Honey in My Heart...

There's a poem by Antonio Machado that goes:

I dreamt last night,
oh marvelous error,
that there were honeybees in my heart,
making honey out of my old failures.

There are enough old failures, old hurts and old pains in my heart to keep a hive of bees busy for awhile.

Growing up in a dysfunctional, toxic society definitely affects one's perspective and one's emotional state. I was no exception.

As Friedrich Nietzsche said, what doesn't destroy you makes you stronger. But, sometimes, you get stronger in ways that may not be good for oneself or for society. The emotional scar tissue can get in the way of future growth.

I experienced the casual, ubiquitous and grindingly demeaning racism and classism of the '50's and '60's. White storekeepers who refused to wait on me until all of the white patrons had been satisfied. School administrators who steered me away from college prep courses because black kids on welfare simply did not go to college, even with unusually high IQ scores. They thought they were doing me a favor.

This type of behavior, experienced at a young age, leads to feelings of rejection, anger and inferiority. My desire to escape led to addictive behavior, including alcohol and drugs. In Camden, self-destructive behavior is considered "normal".

Living in an overly urbanized environment like Camden lead me to believe that the world was man-made. I was born, raised on and surrounded by concrete. I was in my teens before I saw more than ten trees in one place. I lived in a city of concrete, bordered by a river so toxic that it contained no life forms whatsoever. Bacteria would not grow in it. I was a product of the hype of the times – all good things were man-made. Plastic was a wonder. Nuclear power would give us so much energy it would be "too cheap to meter". Processed food was better than natural.

I was the perfect "Breaker"". Afraid of myself, afraid of others, afraid of Nature. Angry and violent, but unclear why. Self medicated. And, I wanted to cure those fears by being in CONTROL.

However, once I learned to release the desire to control the world/events, I gained two things that had eluded me for decades:

- Myself
- The World

As a child stutterer, I learned that I had to choose my words carefully. I learned the

<u>power</u> of words. I led my first demonstration, for better housing in Camden, NJ, when I was 12 years old. Watching people coming out of their houses to join in the demonstration, I learned the power of words to move people to take action.

As a frail, sickly boy in a brutal, violent environment, I learned the value of forging unlikely alliances. I learned to do homework for some of the most violent thugs in the Camden school system – in exchange for protection from the other violent thugs. (Doing their homework posed interesting difficulties for me. I couldn't just copy my answers... they would get 'A's, a sure sign it wasn't their work. It is amazingly hard to formulate realistically wrong answers when you know the right ones.)

As a world traveler and bridge between social/ cultural and spiritual realities, I have learned to look beyond the limitations of one culture. Every single culture has something to offer to every other single culture. Not by blending all cultures into an incomprehensible goo, but by allowing the good and ignoring the rest.

The Evolution of the Spirit

Our Spirits have never evolved. They arise fully formed and developed, have always been and will always be. My Spirit, like yours, is eternal.

But... getting "me" out of the way so that I can SEE this has been a constant challenge! I can get so hung up in what is happening in the world, with my ego, my fears, my desires... that it's hard to hear the Voice of the Spirit within.

No, your "Spirit" does not evolve. Neither does mine nor anyone else's. But, what does evolve, what learns how to get out of the way, is your Personality.

If your Spirit is like your hand, your Personality is a glove fitting over your hand. Our task is to thin our Personality as thin as surgeon's gloves, so thin the hand can pick up a dime.

Most of us in this society are wearing boxing gloves.

My challenge (our challenge) is to SEE ourselves as spiritual beings in the midst of our Earth-walk. To rid ourselves of our blinders (our fears, delusions, limiting thoughts, desires, addictions).

There are a lot of people who profess to be able to help you do this. A whole growth industry has sprung up, called "personal growth and development". Our spiritual starvation, our hunger for Divine connection, drives much of this activity. Some of it is actually legitimate, and can be helpful in moving one along their life path. I can personally attest to this.

And, unfortunately, many people stop right there. In the guise of "growth", they stay stuck, not evolving beyond making their own personal lives more comfortable.

I encourage you to go further – to match your spiritual values with what you see in the world.

To match your personal growth with society's transformation. To make your politics and economics consistent with your inner values.

I offer you a bridge...

The purpose of a bridge is to get you safely from one side of a void to another. A bridge can be as wide as a multi-lane highway. A bridge can be a single cable. Regardless of size, the concept of a bridge is simple:

- You are here.

- You want to be there.

A bridge has value only when it takes you where you want to go. If you are going nowhere, there is no need for a bridge. If everything is fine with you, you have no need for a bridge (or this book). If, however, you perceive through the eyes of inclusivity, that what happens to one of us happens to all of us, you will see that we humans DEFINITELY need to be on the other side of the bridge.

I offer you a goal...

We have created a toxic global human society. However, many choose not to be aware of its toxicity. Many actually revel in it. For them, their goal is simple:

- We are here, and WE WANT to STAY here.

This book is not for them.

There is no such thing as a one-sided bridge. For those who feel in their hearts the necessity to change, I offer these twinned and complementary goals:

- Avoiding the "Default Option": the experience, in our lifetimes, of human overshoot, die-back and the possibility of human extinction on Earth.
- Embracing the experience of the next step in human evolution: *homo sapiens holonus*, the birth of a holistic global human family.

> None of us will make it,
> unless ALL of us make it.

To achieve these goals, to cross the bridge, there is much baggage we must leave behind:

War; poverty; addiction to money; famine; disease; waste; violence; hatred; population explosion; suicide; holes in the ozone layer; political corruption; homelessness; emotional stress; destruction of cultures; overgrazing; use of children as combatants in warfare; violent political conflict; spiritual emptiness; acid rain; pandemics; decline in basic values; teenage pregnancy; increasing disparities in wealth; racism; wage slavery; chemical, biological, nuclear, and other weapons of mass destruction; AIDS; ethnic unrest and conflict; civil wars; public school violence; spreading desertification; political and social alienation; extinction of species; sexism; overuse of chemical fertilizers and pesticides; expanding global corporatism; global climate change; destruction of family life; colonialism and neocolonialism; homicide; political apathy and malaise; attention deficit and other mental disorders in children; terrorism; unsustainability in all aspects of life; genetic manipulation and ownership; militarization of outer space; genocide; cancer - especially in children; economic and class disparities; war between nations; overconsumption; urban deterioration; regional famines; destruction of the natural environment; crime; child slave labor; industrial pollution...

We cannot make it across the bridge while holding on to this baggage. It is time to let it go.

I offer you a life...

For more than half of our human family, "life" means struggling for the bare necessities of life – food, shelter, enough energy to stay warm or to cook food. For more than half of the human family, "life" means suffering, struggle and a future that is at best bleak.

The other half of our human family is over-weight, over-stimulated, over-entertained, over-stressed. Many suffer from the soul-emptiness that leads to addictive behaviors, from drugs to television-watching.

The leading cause of violent death on this

planet is NOT war or homicide. It's suicide. In increasing numbers, our human family embraces suicide as the way out of an empty, meaningless life.

This brutal way of life did not occur by accident. It is the result of a form of human consciousness. That consciousness is TERMINAL on this planet. The good news: we don't have to be terminal with it. We can (and will) change our consciousness.

People are suffering and in pain, because they are waiting for YOU to act. The two sides of the human family know about each other. The side that struggles to find a dollar or two for daily food knows about the side that spends twice that for a cup of coffee. The side that struggles to find clean water knows about the side that flushes the toilet with drinkable water.

In the face of this, I am offering you an alternative to struggle and emptiness.

I offer you transformation…
Yes, things must change. But, how?

Many of our current actions form the beginning of a new way of living, based on a new form of consciousness. Many of us are taking the first steps, in our attempt to live sustainable, ecological and spiritually conscious lives.

The purpose of this book is to make these emerging behaviors coherent, explicit, reinforcing and deep. My purpose is to form the skeleton, the system, from which these emerging behaviors begin to make sense and gain power. My purpose is to spread the new form of consciousness to every single human being on this planet. Together, we can catalyze the global human awakening.

I offer you "Plan B" Change...

Who am I? I'm a "change agent" for a very specific type of transformation. I'm a social/cultural/spiritual transformationist, bridging our societal reality on the one hand with our spiritual and moral principles on the other.

I am about change. You may have heard that line before, most notably from our President, Barack Obama. Both of us are committed to change (as are you). Both of us try to live our values and to bridge gaps in our society. But, what makes our paths so different?

The difference between us is the difference between Plan A and Plan B.

Plan A: Things are basically okay. The center holds. The recent problems are a momentary blip. Our job is to work back to "normal", so that everything can be okay again.

Plan A (with modifications): Things are basically okay. The center holds. We just need to make a few modifications and adjustments to my main issue (health care or gay marriage or gun rights or global climate change...), then everything will be okay again.

Plan B: We've hit an iceberg. It's an iceberg of our own creation. We're going down. The builders of this particular ship didn't even bother putting in any lifeboats. Our only hope is that the ship is going down slowly enough so that we can build our own lifeboats.

"Plan B" is based on a premise: What happens when something that is "too big to fail"... does?

In the movie "Titanic", I think the most important scene is when the owner, the chief engineer and the Captain are talking right after the iceberg hit. Except for some ice chunks on the deck, there is no visible damage. The chief engineer is trying to convince the other two that the ship is going to sink. They think he's crazy. The owner says, "That's impossible! This ship can't sink!"

A crucial point: this is NOT DENIAL. This is an inability to grasp what lies outside of one's consciousness. Saying that our entire society may fail and that we have to transform the way we live is, for some people, akin to saying, "Gravity's going to shut off next year and you'd better be tied down when that happens!"

A mind that's flexible and adaptable enough to understand and encompass the concepts in this book is on a different evolutionary plane than one that thinks the status quo is "okay" or "inevitable", and that our organizations and institutions "cannot fail". This does not mean that one person is "good" and another "bad". It does mean that one is more *appropriate* than the other, from the vantage point of the future.

I believe our President is both intelligent and authentic. I know he'll get around to "Plan B" thinking eventually… and hopefully, in time to help with the lifeboats.

I offer you MY life…

My life, just like yours, has a trajectory. I was born, I live, I will die. What we DO between the living and dying becomes the measure and meaning of our lives.

I am fully aware that, in this violent world, there are some who may want to attack me for some of the things I say in this book. Some may see the call for transformation as a threat to their religion, their means of making money, their political system (or all three). I realize that some are so separated that they may want to physically harm me.

I could play it "safe". Not say certain things. Not write this book at all.

But, we are not born into this life to "play it safe". We are not on this planet to practice SAFETY; we are here to practice COMPASSION, to live a meaningful, Spirit-filled life.

Each of you, every one of us, will die. That's a given. When that moment comes (as it may today, for all we know), the important question is whether or not you fulfilled your life's purpose, whether you brought healing, compassion and awakening to the world. And yourself.

At the end of your days on Earth, you do face a Judge. It's YOU.

We have been toxifying the
Earth and killing one another
for the last 8,000 years of
human history.

This moment is coming to an
abrupt end.

Whether we end with the
moment ~ or evolve to the next
step for humanity ~ is up to us.

SEED #2:
SEEING THE PROBLEM

We must see the plain truth of this moment,
if we wish to survive.

Without seeing, thoroughly understanding, and discussing the real problems, we create solutions to minor problems (or non-problems) and we propose solutions that are not as profound as the problem they are designed to address.

"We are essentially throwing our children into furnaces to heat and light [our present] homes."

Albert Bates

We have created a toxic way of living
on this planet.

We constantly and routinely break our relationships with the Earth, break our relationships with all of the plants and animals, break our relationships with other humans, break our relationships with our own inner being. We break our relationship with the Divine/Transcendent.

We have mutually convinced ourselves that
this is the best and only way to live.

The Breaker Culture gets crammed into us, non-stop, constantly. Every advertisement we see, every news program we hear, every step down every street – we marinate in this hyper-culture.

But, Breaker Culture has been at work, well before America hit the "on" switch after World War II. For thousands of years, this consciousness has been touted as the best (and only) possible way that humans can live on this planet.

Mainstream religion is a primary tool for keeping things as they have been. Religion has been used as the explainer and justifier of the status quo – even when it is toxic, cruel or downright absurd. And those who dare say that the religious leaders are in violation of Universal Principles get their heads chopped off (John the Baptist), nailed to crosses (Jesus of Nazareth), flogged, flayed, burned alive... Anything to maintain the Breaker point of view, Breaker domination and Breaker control.

... our future is like that of the passengers of a small pleasure boat sailing quietly above the Niagara Falls...

James Lovelock

We refer to our destructive, addictive, paranoid and toxic lives as "human nature". It is not.

We revel in needless violence, despite the lessons of the wise. We derive our identity, our values and our entertainment from the things our wisdom teachers warn us against.

Lovelock's Musical Chairs:
According to James Lovelock, we're about to play a strange game of musical chairs. There are 30 people circling in the room. The game starts with two chairs available. When the music stops, everyone without a chair dies.

For 8,000 years, we have created societies of broken and breaking people. This is the Breaker legacy.

In 8,000 years, we have created a global human society that is terminal. It doesn't matter how it started. After 80 centuries, what created this fundamental shift in human behavior is immaterial. What is important is *how* to change, *right now*.

However, there is another way.

The Stakes are High: The Default Option is… We Don't Make It.

Dr. James Lovelock, the scientist who came up with the "Gaia Hypothesis", recently made a prediction, based on his decades of research on planetary climate change. He said that by the dawn of the 22nd Century, less than 100 years from now, virtually all humans on the planet will die. He said that humankind will consist of at most 200 million people, living in the Arctic Circle, as the only spot on the planet that can continue to support human life. The rest of the planet will look like Mars. The planet will eventually come back, but *without us.*

The "Gaia Hypothesis": the scientific explanation of what Keepers have always known: that the Earth is one living being and all living beings are an integral part of the Earth as a Being.

Lovelock's prediction goes one step further. He said that the point of no return, where the damage becomes inevitable, was reached 15 years ago.

Breaker Consciousness Created This Mess.

…there is a chance that nothing we can do can now stop Earth from being reduced to a lifeless desert world like Mars, perhaps even within the lifetime of some of those now alive…

Albert Bates

All of us see this consciousness at work. We have given names to parts and fragments of this consciousness. We have called this consciousness and its manifestations many things: slavery, colonialism, the white power structure, the patriarchy.

None of these partial labels fit. There were always people identified as the villains who weren't villains themselves, getting lumped in with the villains because they were the "wrong" skin color, gender, religion…. And there were always people identified with the victims who were in fact villains, getting a "pass" because they shared the victims' skin color, gender, religion...

We can't look at a person's skin color, genitalia, age, nationality or any other external circumstance to ascertain his inward state or true nature.

We must learn to look beyond that.

My term "Breaker" identifies a person's consciousness and behavior, not her condition. Anyone, at any time, can act as a Breaker. And, anyone, at any time, can <u>cease</u> behaving as a Breaker. It only takes a shift of mind and heart.

An Immoral Society

A city that spends millions building a brand new "house" for a sports team (one that already had a functioning structure), while leaving thousands of humans to wander its streets, cold, lonely, sick and homeless... is an immoral city. That is an immoral choice. The fact that it was made by seemingly sensible, apparently intelligent people does not make it less immoral.

Any society that forces a parent to choose between feeding his children and keeping a roof over their heads is an immoral society.

Any society that forces a young girl to choose between starvation for her family or prostituting her body is an immoral society.

In a society as rich as America, when large numbers of people go without basic health care, that, too is a sign of an immoral society.

The Purpose of Breaker Consciousness
There is another way to look at all this. There is a purpose and meaning to this present Mess.

The Mess is a necessary stimulus for humanity to evolve to its next step.

Breaker consciousness created this Mess. Paradoxically, by ending this Mess, Menders will develop both a planetary outlook/ worldview and a planetary operating system that can effectively dismantle and disenchant the Breaker Operating System. Our present conditions will force us to evolve.

Breaker consciousness forms the "shell" around the emerging Mender consciousness.

Your doctor must have a broken leg to heal. Your defects are the ways that glory gets manifested. Whoever sees clear what's dis-eased in himself begins to gallop on The Way. There is nothing worse than thinking you are well enough. And don't believe for a moment that you're healing yourself.

Rumi

This has been our time of incubation. Now, it is time to crack open the shell – from the inside. It is time to set the shell aside. It is time for a real breakthrough.

Some chicks don't hatch. They aren't strong enough, or the shell is too tough, or the shell isn't tough enough and breaks before the chick is fully formed.

Or, the chick just doesn't know how to crack the shell.

Or, the chick doesn't believe cracking the shell is important. It's comfortable where it is. It is content in its "comfort zone" — for now.

I have faith.

That...

- Despite the tough shell of the Breaker Mess, that we Menders are tougher.

- We Menders are fully equipped with everything necessary for our next step. We don't need space aliens or disembodied characters to "save" us. (Although all help is welcome!)

- In the face of our concerted action, the seemingly desperate conditions we face WILL CHANGE. Those conditions will stop being so fearful when we chose to stop being afraid.

What would happen if we consciously created human societies that are based on the core values of our wisdom teachers?

What would happen if we dedicated our lives and our societies to healing the Mess that the Breakers left behind?

What would happen if we healed our human relations, clearing our nations and our hearts of violence, hatred and the illusion of separation?

What would happen if we replaced the love of money and the love of violence with a different set of values – and then ACTED on those values?

HOW WOULD SUCH A SOCIETY OPERATE?

SEED #3:
THE SOLUTION

We must become the Menders.

If humans will be living on this planet, we must mend. We must mend all of the ways our Breaker behaviors have damaged and broken us and the Earth.

To do this kind of healing, we must adopt a fundamentally different view of reality. Everything must be re-examined, questioned and re-thought.

We must adopt a "Mender" worldview. The Mender worldview is not "new". It is 1,000,000 years old. It is the worldview of the Keepers.

Menders take the intensely local worldview and values of the Keepers and apply them to the entire planet, including other humans in other areas. Menders will form the world's first global human society.

We Are Wired For Relationship

We are hard-wired to be in relationship with ourselves, all other beings, with the Web of Life and with the Divine. It is etched into our DNA (the parts that Breaker scientists refer to as "junk" DNA).

But, we must do more than think and talk. We must act.

To conquer the Earth is to destroy ourselves as well as everything else. If human beings were to discover their interconnectedness with the Earth, and realize that we are inextricably imbedded in the Earth, then the technology and the cleverness certainly exists to solve these problems. It's really only a change of heart that's required. This may seem huge, but on the other hand, that's all that's required -- only a change of heart.

John Seed

The Vision: A World That Works for All

A significant portion of the earth's population will soon recognize, if they haven't already done so, that humanity is now faced with a stark choice: Evolve or die.

Eckhart Tolle

If we shift quickly enough, we will witness the beginning of a transformation that will bring both the Earth and our planetary human family into harmony.

But, this vision won't happen without a plan.

This is such a plan.

The Evolution: Homo Sapiens Holonus

It is time for us to evolve.

To achieve the transformation, we must become more than homo sapiens, the "thinking man". We are diverging into two sub-species: *homo sapiens separatus* and *homo sapiens holonus*. The humans who think they are separate and the humans who recognize they are one with All.

Only *one* of these species is viable.

The Forces of Evolution

The evolution from *separatus* to *holonus* is taking place in the human mind and heart. *Holonus* is an adaptation to a hostile environment – an environment created and maintained by separatus.

Transforming human consciousness...

There are simply hundreds of books,

videos, practices, methodologies that talk about transforming or expanding human consciousness. Many of them are sincere, authentic and valuable. Still others are redundant or simply flaky.

...for the purpose of transforming human behavior...

But, we must ask ourselves: WHY are we interested in transforming human consciousness? Is this a sincere desire of awakening, or a "Breaker" desire to get more "stuff", to get an advantage over the competition, to appear "better than", to "have it all"?

...for the purpose of transforming human culture...

The purpose of changing human consciousness is to change human behavior. The purpose of that transformation is to beneficially influence and heal all human cultures and societies, and to heal human impacts on all other beings. In short, the purpose of transforming human culture is to create a world that works for all beings.

...for the purpose of transforming the Earth.

All of this transformation has one goal: the evolution of humanity as an integral step toward the transformation of the Earth, from suffering what Lovelock calls a planetary "morbid fever" to a green oasis where all life forms can survive and thrive. We are an integral step in the transformation from Earth to Gaia, a self-aware planetary being – with humans acting like her neural network (instead of cancer cells).

Anything short of this goal of transformation is self-serving and does not have sufficient transformative value to get us out of the Mess we are in.

Without clearly articulating and practicing our primary operative values (the ones we live, not the ones we just talk about), we fall in danger of slipping back into the default Breaker values.

SEED #4:
PRINCIPLES AND VALUES

What is the Source of Wisdom?

There are three sources for authentic wisdom teachings and our universal human values:

#3. One way is in the lessons and guidance of those we refer to as the wisdom teachers. This is the LEAST powerful way to obtain wisdom – but still effective.

#2. Another source of wisdom can be found in the Order of the Universe and in the Web of Life itself, a dynamic equilibrium that constantly renews, heals, feeds and balances. A better way to understand the laws of Life is to observe Life itself.

#1. The primary source for wisdom is what lies in your own Heart. You, indeed each one of us, have a direct connection to the Divine.

Breaker Culture distorts the wisdom teachings, ignores the Laws of Life and gets you to mistrust and disconnect from your own heart.

President George W. Bush, on his knees in the White House, prays for guidance from God. A powerful voice inside told to invade Afghanistan and Iraq.

Osama bin Laden, on his knees in a deep cave in Pakistan, prays for guidance from God. He is told to bomb the World Trade Center and to commit other acts of terrorism.

Both of them received exactly opposing guidance. They both thought they were talking to God. Neither one of them was talking to God.

Internal voices can be very powerful. And very wrong.

The reason for this three-part source of wisdom is simple. This is a system of Divine "checks and balances". If all three sources say the same thing, you can be sure you're dealing with a universal law.

If you see conflict between any of these three sources, you know either:

1. You aren't paying attention.
2. You aren't interpreting correctly.
3. Something is being distorted (or missed).

The Failure of "Religion"

People are "atheists" because of what "religionists" have done to the wisdom teachings.

- A Buddha statue is just a piece of rock with some carvings.
- A Qur'an is just some paper with scratchings.
- A Crucifix is just a piece of jewelry or a wall hanging.

These are meaningless outward symbols. They only become relevant when the underlying meaning and values are PRACTICED.

- A "Buddhist" government turns away a ship filled with compassionate relief supplies, intended for innocent civilians being imprisoned... by the "Buddhist" government.
- A "Muslim" recites words from the Qur'an in prayer... then loads a car full of explosives, set to kill men, women and children...

reciting the same lines from the Qur'an in prayer.
- A "Christian", claiming to uphold the sanctity of life, destroys the life of an abortion provider.

We need something MORE. Religion is just not enough…

We live in a world where religion has been hijacked.

Karen Armstrong

"Religion" or Operating System?

Your "religion" is what you do in church (or temple, mosque…) when you think everyone is looking.

Your "operating system" is how you behave the rest of the time, when you think no one is looking, or when you're sleep-walking through life, acting without thinking, acting the way you see others around you acting, acting as though there are no consequences.

How many observe Christ's Birthday -- how few Christ's teachings.

Benjamin Franklin

The Breaker Operating System is at odds with most of the wisdom teachings. When there is conflict, when there is desire for power and control, the wisdom teachings get tossed aside.

What are Humanity's Universal Values?

I have read all of the "holy books" attributed to all of the significant wisdom teachers. I have read <u>across</u> them, rather than focusing exclusively on one. It is an attitude of *exclusivity* that causes us to be blind to the commonalities among the wisdom traditions. The wisdom teachers were all saying the same thing. They could say nothing else – All wisdom is One.

We can develop a society based on the 10

Universal Principles/Values:
1.   Love/Agape/Metta (loving-kindness)
2.   Peace/Ahimsa/Nonviolence/Dra-la
3.   Compassion/Service/Dana/Neighbor-
liness (caring for others)
4.   Forgiveness/Tolerance/Karma
5.   Patience/Humility/Surrender
6.   Golden Rule/Inclusivity/Equanimity
7.   Righteousness/Dharma/Truth/Tao/
Authenticity/Purity
8.   Joy/Gratitude
9.   Responsibility/Empowerment/Action
    • Individual
    • Collective
10.   Awakened Consciousness

Obviously, any discussion of any one of the above ten principles would take a book. And, there will be some who come up with better words than I use here, or question whether one concept belongs on the same line with another. This is the *start* of a dialog on our universal principles, not the *completion*.

The point here is to introduce the basic concept: our values are not held by any ONE religion or wisdom tradition, but by ALL of them. Viewed together, we can see our foundational values – what makes us truly human.

Relational consciousness unites us with our universal values.

We all believe and value the same things.

It's time to realize this.

Universal Values – Connecting the Jigsaw Puzzle Pieces

The jigsaw puzzle: the concept of relational consciousness honors all paths to the Divine. Each and every wisdom teacher brought expressions of the Truth – through the filter of their own lives, their own culture, the particular times they were born into and their own experiences. This is the only way the teaching could be relevant for the times. Not only are all of the wisdom teachers relevant and correct, the process of revelation itself was necessary for the evolution of humanity.

In order to become one people, one humanity, every group, culture, people must contribute something. We arrive at this point of evolution when we can see that all of the wisdom teachings fit together, like the pieces of a jigsaw puzzle. The curve of one puzzle piece fits the contour of the other.

Each piece can be seen on its own. Each piece contains a fairly coherent picture. But, each piece contributes to a larger picture, to the understanding of the whole. Each piece is incomplete without each and every other piece. None of us sees the totality of the Truth. But together, we can all help each other to see.

To see and learn this, we needed to evolve to a species that spanned the globe, that spent more time talking and comparing notes than killing each other – a species that realized that *relating* to each other was more important than *competing* with, dominating and controlling each other. This species is ready for the next step. That's us.

Our Primary Value Lies in Honoring the Web of Life.

Before newborn babies are fully coordinated, they will punch themselves, scratch their eyes, bite their fingers... Then they learn to coordinate all the parts of its body. It discovers that it's <u>one being</u>. It comes into its oneness.

There are two operative primary values at work on our planet right now: a Breaker value and a Keeper/Mender value.

The Breaker value is "The Primacy of Self". "I" come first, and every other species (including other humans) is subservient to "my" wants, needs and desires. This value is suicidal and biocidal. It has led to our perilous moment on this planet.

The Keeper/Mender value is "The Primacy of the Web of Life". It is the central imperative of all life. It is the one key thing that Breakers do not understand.

The Web of Life is known by many names in many cultures: Tao, Integral Way, The Path, the City of God, the Presence.

The Wisdom Teachings

All of our wisdom teachers taught the same thing. They taught the sacred, interconnected Web of Life. They came out sounding different, because of differences in time, language, culture and conditions, but they all pointed to the existence of a higher power, a higher purpose and a greater human potential.

We are creating an operating
system that honors, harmonizes
and integrates the hopes,
the values and worldview
of the Keepers with our
current complex, global and
technological point of view.

We are creating a way for all
of us, for all beings, to relate to
each other and to relate to the
Earth as a whole.

The world cannot be healed by the Breaker thinking that caused the problems in the first place.

The Earth cannot be healed by good talk, good intentions, questing for higher consciousness or hoping for the best. Yes, all of these things, and more, are necessary. However...

We must ACT, with focus, commitment and vision. We must act together.

This is our action plan. This is our operating system.

SEED #5:
THE OPERATING SYSTEM

A **VISION** is the roadmap to where we're going. An **OPERATING SYSTEM** is the vehicle, the methodology of how we're going to get there.

In order to act, we need a pattern, a model, a framework, a vehicle, a language, a plan -- in other words, we need an operating system.

What is an Operating System?
Without an operating system, a computer is a really big doorstop. A very expensive way to put a blinking cursor on a monitor.

Our society consists of what we do, and how we do it. Our society consists of our collective actions. Our "operating system" consists of the millions of interconnected decisions and acts that make up everyday living.

And, just like the operating system on your computer, most of the time it operates in the background, automatically, beneath our conscious awareness. You don't think about society's operating system... until something goes wrong.

... a failure to see is the biggest barrier towards tackling our challenges. The dilemma we're faced with in coping with the modern world is that things are so complex and so fast moving that it's very difficult to get a picture of the whole: it's very difficult to see.

Otto Scharmer

The Need for a New Operating System
Communism and Capitalism are two branches from the same poisonous tree of exclusivity and the illusion of separation. We need a new tree.

All political ideologies based on Breaker thinking assert that humans are essentially materialists – that our highest good lies in producing and consuming "stuff".

Everything we identify that is toxic in American society stems from the "capitalist" version of the Breaker Operating System. Everything that early dissident and former Czech President Vaclav Havel identified as toxic in the former Soviet empire stemmed from the "communist" version of the Breaker Operating System. Same operating system, different manifesting toxicity.

The Failure of Imagination

We are so conditioned by and familiar with the Breaker Operating System, many of us take it to be "reality". We simply cannot imagine a world that could operate without an economic system we call "capitalism" (or "communism" or "socialism"...) and without a political system we call "democracy" and a religious/belief system we call "Christianity" (or "Islam" or "Buddhism" or "Judaism" or "Hinduism"...)

In fact, the Breaker Operating System has morphed well beyond all of those ideological labels. We frankly don't know what it is anymore, and many of us frankly don't care – so long as the system works... for ME.

But, imagine we must, for the Breaker system has reached its terminus... it's about to plunge over the cliff... and it is carrying us along with it.

Reality is that which, when you stop believing in it, doesn't go away.

Phillip K. Dick

Instead of believing in the rapture, or in rescue by benevolent space aliens, it is time for us to believe in ourselves.

You can't depend on your eyes when your imagination is out of focus.

Mark Twain

The Breaker Operating Systems (capitalism, communism, socialism, democracy, monarchy, feudalism, even anarchy) are all built upon the toxic Breaker platform of exclusivity, unconsciousness and separation.

If society fits you comfortably enough, you call it freedom.

Robert Frost

A Script for 6,800,000,000+ Actors

According to Paul Hawken and his "Wiser Earth" initiative, there are millions of people, in over one million organizations, playing their part in healing the Earth.

But, without an operating system, all of our efforts are doomed to failure.

Where there is no vision, the people perish...

Proverbs 29:18 (and, chiseled into the granite of Camden City Hall)

We are creating a Relational
Operating System, one
that honors, harmonizes and
integrates the hopes, the values
and worldview of the Keepers
with our current complex, global
and technological moment in
time.

We are creating a way for all
of us, for all beings, to relate to
each other and to relate to the
Earth as a whole.

The good news: with the
Relational Operating System,
we stand on the threshold of our
success.

The Three Circles Analysis – the Essence of Human Society

We cannot change society unless we understand it. And we cannot begin to understand it with our overly complex analytical tools taught in most major universities. They prevent us from seeing the simple truth.

We cannot change human societies by believing that any ONE society is representative of ALL.

What can we say that is true regarding virtually every human society? What are the essential elements of human societies?

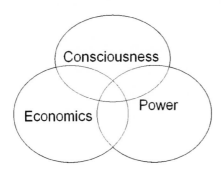

There are three principal factors that interact to make any society:

- **Consciousness**: How we experience ourselves, our inner being, our spiritual lives, our interactions with others. Our worldview.
- **Economics:** How we maintain our physical existence and satisfy our basic needs.
- **Power:** How we govern our own and others' behaviors for the common good. (Another way to think about power is the term "politics". However, in this society, most of us wrongfully think that politics is just "voting", when it is much more.)

These three factors exist in EVERY human society. How they interact determines whether a society is dysfunctional or healthy.

A dysfunctional, adversarial society, a Breaker society, is comprised of these dysfunctional elements:

The Consciousness of Fear, Scarcity and Separation

- Spiritual starvation and decadence, moral decay, ignorance.
- "Us-vs.-Them" thinking supporting racism, sexism, bigotry and hatred.
- Consciousness of pain and lack, leading to suffering, anger and violence.
- A feeling of having no future (or an apocalyptic "Mad Max" future), leading to anger, depression, despair and violence.

The Economics of Greed and Poverty

- Poverty creates an atmosphere of inferiority, depression, stress and despair.
- Gap between rich and poor leads to greed, envy and violence.
- Promotion of non-sustainable, addiction-building lifestyles.

Anybody who believes exponential growth can go on forever in a finite world is either a madman or an economist.

Kenneth Boulding

Power: The Leadership of the Elite

- Power in the hands of elites; ordinary people have little power to change their lives.
- Violence used to gain or keep power - or as a source of empty entertainment.

People use political ideas to hurt and fight each other, ... it is not a dedication to the hungry or the poor, but to an ideology which would make each man the enemy of the one who does not think as he does.

Anais Nin

This is the kind of society that most humans are familiar with. It is the dominant operating system of our planet at this time. This is the Breaker Operating System.

It doesn't have to be this way.

A healthy, inclusive, relational society, a Keeper or Mender society, is comprised of these functional elements:

Awakening, Integrating Consciousness
- Spiritual awakening; moral development; awareness expansion.
- "We are one" thinking that leads to inclusivity in action.
- Consciousness of mutual service leading to compassionate action.

- A clear vision of a positive future, leading to a sense of belonging and meaning.

Economics Honoring the Web of Life

- A society where all basic needs are met.
- Sense of "enoughness" closes gap between rich and poor.
- Promotion of sustainable lifestyles.
- Healing and sustaining the Earth and healing relationships between all beings, including humans.

The Power of Emergence

- People have power over their lives and their destiny (not distant government or elite groups).
- Democratic power at the most local level.
- Violence not a tool of power gain or manipulation.

The Benefits of a Relational Operating System

To heal the world, we Menders must create a *relational* operating system. A Relational Operating System assumes that our relationships are paramount to every other possible consideration (including and especially money).

We will evolve the intensely local value system and worldview of the Keepers into a global and complex human society, on a thriving Earth.

A Vision of a Healing World

With a healing, functional, Relational Operating System in place, we can then begin to envision true healing on our planet. Our visions would include:

Consciousness

Vision: Aware and awakened individuals, communities, nations and world, acting in accordance with universal and human principles, expressing and exchanging gifts, skills and service. An end to human adversarial relationships.

Economics

Vision: An alternative, complementary and sustainable economic system, with humans motivated by the experience of fulfillment, abundant love, compassion, community and relationship, not the acquisition of more money.

Power

Vision: A locally-led, distributed network of empowered people and empowered, consensual, self-directed communities, focused on bringing healing to the local environments in which we live and balance to the Earth.

The Role of Culture in the 3 Circles Analysis

Culture is the primary transmission vehicle for each of the Three Circles. Culture is the bed upon which the 3 Circles rest, the ocean within which we all swim. Culture keeps societies stable – consciousness, economics and power may be the engines, but culture is the shock absorber. It is virtually impossible to conceive of humans outside of culture. So, to speak of changing (for example) our Economics from

Breaker to Relational, that transformation can only occur within the context of our CULTURE of economic activity.

Changing our culture is both a challenge and an opportunity.

The challenge: Breaker media focuses our attention on the hyper-inflated economy of the super-rich (what I call the "Red Market"). But, most economic activity takes place at the level of ordinary humans – us. So, the challenge for us is learning to recognize and activate our real economic power, and to stop paying attention to the media-fueled Red Market.

The opportunity: to consciously direct our economy. To stop buying mindlessly, reacting as we are programmed and conditioned. To choose where to place our economic power and resources.

To perceive the need, the vision and the benefit of the Relational Operating System, we need to adopt a relational consciousness.

"Relational Consciousness" means being in conscious relationship with all, and acting accordingly.

The Role of Consciousness in the Relational Operating System

Each of us, every living being on this planet, is hard-wired for a direct experience of the Divine. It is as vital to being as eating and sleeping, as the experience of joy and pain.

For thousands of years, our wisdom teachers have pointed toward this Divine relationship, our connection to the Sacred. This is the latest pointing, at the dawn of the great turning.

Knowing that people don't really eat them, some bakers make parts of their wedding cakes out of Styrofoam.

Seeking spiritual fulfillment in a Breaker society is like trying to draw nourishment from a Styrofoam wedding cake. Just because it's called "cake" doesn't mean it is. Just because you eat it doesn't mean it's good for you. Just because you eat it doesn't mean it's food.

Breakers and the Consciousness of Separation

Breakers have broken the essential relationship. In doing so, Breakers have created societies that are spiritually empty and unfulfilling, populated with spiritually starved people.

Breaker Consciousness destroys the sacred relationship by denying the sacredness that is all around us, by turning the Divine into an abstraction. They do so by promoting "God" as a means of controlling other humans and as an excuse and justification for their own destructive behavior.

Menders: Restoring the Consciousness of Inclusivity

Those of us operating with Mender Consciousness are restoring our relationship with the Divine – by

*The ocean
is still the ocean...
regardless of the
drop's philosophy*

Rumi

restoring our relationships with each other, with all other beings and with the Earth. In doing so, Menders are creating a spirit-fulfilling, meaningful, magical, sacred society.

Relational consciousness honors and connects with historic religious traditions and cultures, but frees us from useless and inappropriate (and internally conflicting) dogma. The forms may remain the same, but the behaviors can change. (Even the forms may change – for example, Catholics moving the altar to the center of gathered worshippers, after about 2,000 years.)

Relational consciousness searches for commonalities, not for reasons for separation. By comparing wisdom traditions and encouraging religion to evolve, we can leave behind confusing, conflicting, dogmatic and just inappropriate aspects – both within and between wisdom teachings.

Economics is the management and allocation of abundances.

To do this, we must be in harmonious and authentic relationship with each other, and with the Earth.

This is what we call "Relational Economics"

The Role of Economics in the Relational Operating System

The Essence of Economics

The management of abundance? This is the exact OPPOSITE of what is taught in college. College professors, on the first day of the first economics class, say, "Economics is the management and allocation of SCARCITY". He (or she) then taught you how to be in an adversarial and competitive relationship with other human beings and to see the Earth as a source of resources to be exploited without consequence.

From this position of scarcity, lack and separation, we create Breaker economic systems – me against you, my group against your group, all of us using up the Earth and Her resources as fast as we can.

What happens when we start from a radically different perspective? What happens if we start with an Earth that grows enough food, that receives enough energy, that has enough of everything we need (even though it may not have enough for everything we can fantasize about)?

What is "Relational Economics?"

Simply put, it is any economic system that replaces adversarial and self-centered economic behavior with an understanding of the primacy and sacredness of the Web of Life. The purpose of Relational Economics is maintaining and enhancing relationships with all beings.

If there is enough for all, the most important thing in economics is building cooperative relationships between the participants in the economy – to insure that there will continue to be enough for all. (We call this "sustainability".)

The Exchange

Each of us, every being on this planet, is an integral part of "The Exchange", the vast flow of abundances that constitutes the Web of Life.

Humans have engaged in this Exchange for almost 1,000,000 years. It is still hard-wired in our bodies. The Keepers among us still practice it.

Breaker Economics disrupts the Exchange.

Breakers do so by over-producing, collecting, hoarding beyond all needs. Breaking the sacred relationship with all beings. Blocking and controlling natural flows. Generating and feeding addictive behavior. Considering anyone or anything not immediately and obviously useful to themselves as disposable "waste" and "garbage" -- and treating them accordingly. Enslaving and demeaning all other beings (including human beings) for profit.

Breakers have no respect for the Web of Life –

they cannot even SEE it. They see a collection of individual beings and collectable resources, ready to be exploited. They don't see how it fits together. The Breaker mindset reduces all relationships to commodities – ready to be sold to the highest bidder. (This includes human beings.)

Menders, through Relational Economics, are restoring our place in the planetary Exchange.

10 Key Aspects of Relational Economics:

1. Abundance

God always overdoes everything. The Earth has vast, sustainable resources, in plentiful abundance when the Web of Life is honored and all beings respected.

It is not crazy for us to think about having within our power, uniquely for the first time in the history of the world, the chance to end extreme poverty within a generation. That is what the numbers show.

Jeffrey Sachs

Producing hundreds of apples, thousands of fish and millions of mayflies IS the Web of Life. All life is part of this great Exchange.

Breakers believe they are not.

2. Enoughness

There is enough for all.

That is a fundamental Truth of the Web of Life. The dynamic balance of abundances is a fundamental feature of the Web of Life. Everything produces. Everything consumes. That is how the Web of Life works.

Enoughness means recognizing that security and a sense of well-being and fulfillment comes from *within*, from living in *balance*, not from having and hoarding more "stuff".

Every being on the planet knows how much is enough. Except humans, when we are caught up in Breaker consciousness.

> Abundance doesn't last long when anyone hoards.

A bear takes and eats a salmon from a stream. The bear then defecates in the woods. (Yes, they do.) To the small animals, insects and micro-organisms that feast on the bear's feces, a bear is a food production factory. There is no waste.

The addiction to having MORE creates the craziness that feeds the insecurity inherent within Breaker societies. Examples of this insane behavior include addiction, hoarding, deficit spending, over-production, over-consumption, "more is better" gluttony.

3. The Exchange

Every living being, every dynamic system, is part of the Exchange.

In the Web of Life, EVERYTHING is food for everything else. The Web of Life produces in over-abundance. Through that over-abundance, the Web of Life provides for all.

Trees and other green living things take in sunlight and water. Through a complex process, they absorb what they need to grow, and then give off a toxic, poisonous (for them) gas: oxygen. There is no waste.

For all of human history, Keepers have been an integral part of that Exchange, taking as needed, giving where possible, flowing. For Keepers, there is no "waste". Compassion and joy creates and sustains the Exchange.

Breaker consciousness interrupts the Exchange.

Menders restore and heal the Web of Life by being mindful of and honoring the Exchange.

4. The Means of Production

Karl Marx said that whoever controls the means of production controls the economy and ultimately the society.

He was right.

Marx also said that, if the means of production were in the hands of the wealthy few, it would create a system of greed, corruption, inequality and exploitation.

He was right again.

Marx said that, to insure against these tendencies, economic power should be in the hands of the State.

He was dead wrong.

If we cannot trust the means of production in the hands of a few, or in the hands of the State, who can we trust?

We can trust all of us – together.

We live in a world where the means of production can be in the hands of a local community, applying local values to local conditions. Everyone in the community can be in relationship to the means of production.

This relationship acts as a check on greed, excess, waste and corruption, by keeping the means of production *local* and *transparent*.

Keeping things small, local and relational prevents an exclusive few from amassing and accumulating power by owning and controlling the means of production. This creates a check on abusive power.

Through this shared means of production, relational economics is directly tied to the concept of relational governance.

Examples:
- A micro-electric power plant that powers 20 houses – constructed and run by the people who live in the 20 houses. They all determine how much power to generate, what sources will be used, who operates the system – they "own" the system.
- Intensively (and organically) cultivated land, growing food for the people who are reverently bonded to the land. They all determine what food is grown, when it is planted and harvested, and whether or not chemicals are used in production – they "own" the land.
- A well that supplies a community of 100 – shared by the people of that community. They determine how much water is produced and how it is distributed – they "own" the well.

5. Ownership

Present notions of "ownership" are based on the Breaker consciousness of separation.

For Keepers and Menders, "ownership" is a bundle of RELATIONSHIPS, determined by community norms and needs. (This was the real energy and intention regarding the "sale" of Manhattan Island to the European settlers. For the Keepers, they thought they were making an exchange of value: beads for hunting and fishing rights – the right to *share* the island. The idea of exclusivity -- that they could be excluded from sharing in the use of the land -- was INCONCEIVABLE to them. And, if you look at this as a Mender, it still is inconceivable.)

In Breaker Consciousness, "ownership" is a piece of paper, given in exchange for other pieces of paper, allowing us to do whatever we wish, with few consequences. Some years ago, I worked and lived in a large, 100 year old house here in Portland, with a very large garden, anchored by a 100 year old cedar tree. The cedar was more than anchor for the garden; it was an energy anchor for both the human and the more than human communities surrounding it. Hawks perched on its crown. Raccoons slept by day in its branches. I would sit at its base and meditate.

Some years ago, the property changed hands. And, one of the first things that the new "owner" did was take a chainsaw to the cedar. Why? Who knows. Maybe simply because he could do it.

Mender "ownership" must mean something very different from what it means now. It must represent a responsibility to honor and treat as sacred that with which we are in relationship. A responsibility to *steward*, not a right to *destroy*. A responsibility to ask for permission (of humans and others) before taking such a permanent and devastating action as cutting down a century-old tree.

6. No Poverty/No Extravagance

The practice of enoughness means that a person knows how much is enough and stops eating. This implies that she also knows both how much is too little, and how much is too much.

Having "too little" and having "too much" are two different sides of the same coin: a poverty consciousness. Having too little means one lacks the resources to sustain a meaningful life. Having too much means one lacks the community connections to apply and share one's abundance in a meaningful way, to support the human family and to support the Earth.

7. Right Livelihood

Here's a test: would you perform your present job if you were NOT paid to do so?

Do you work because you ENJOY what you are doing? Because the work is important, vital, significant? Do you work as a way to practice your spirituality? Do you work to make the world a better place?

That's called "right livelihood" or "Mender livelihood".

Conversely: do you work for "money"? Would you stop working if the money stopped? Do you produce or promote toxic elements (or toxic thoughts) in your work? Do you produce or trade in violence and suffering? Does your work hurt other people? Does it hurt beings other than humans? Does it hurt the Earth?

That's referred to as "Breaker livelihood".

8. The Gift Economy

Your life is a Gift from the Divine. What is your gift in return?

- You save a person from a burning building.
- You hold the door for someone.
- You give to your favorite charity.
- You help push a stalled car out of traffic to the side of the road.
- You give some of your favorite homemade jam to a neighbor.

Why do you do these things? What do you get in return?

There is a return. But, it cannot be measured on the scales of Breaker society.

Would you say to the person in the burning building (or the guy who's trying to push his stalled car out of traffic), "I'll help you, but I want money in return." Of course not.

Both of you, Giver and Receiver, are part of the Gift Economy. In the Gift Economy, both giver and receiver are enriched. Any part of the Exchange that is "gain-gain" or "win-win" is an element of the Gift Economy.

9. The Spiritual Economy

You make a temple offering that is burned or otherwise consumed in the offering. You wash the windows of the monastery, or sweep the floor of the church. Your acts of devotion and ritual form another type of transcendental economy, what I call the Spirit Economy.

Both the Gift and Spirit Economies form invisible webs that strengthen and enrich the Web of Life in ways that we cannot begin to understand with our rational minds.

We go to a restaurant, buy food, eat, leave. We have an experience of eating satisfying (and hopefully healthy) food, good atmosphere, pleasing surroundings. We benefit, the restaurant benefits... part of the Exchange.

In the Spiritual Economy, there are also definite (though perhaps harder to quantify) experiences: joy, peace, the Presence of the Divine, spiritual knowing, depth of being... We benefit from these experiences... and the ties to our spiritual community are strengthened. This is the Exchange, but at a more subtle level.

Breakers have banished and outlawed expressions of the Gift and Spirit Economies in Keeper cultures, often by penalty of death. Why? What is so frightening about giving? Why was the practice of the "potlatch" among North American Indians outlawed, punishable by death? What is so frightening about recognizing and honoring the sacred, the Transcendent?

- Loss of Power over Others: The Spirit/Gift Economies acknowledge a Power greater than that of the Breaker Operating Structure

– the Power of Local Community and the Power of the Transcendent/Divine.

- Ignorance: anything that Breakers don't understand is labeled as "wrong", "bad", "evil" or otherwise threatening.
- Weakening the Breaker "god": The Spirit/ Gift Economies minimize the power and value of "money".
- Loss of control: The "profit" in the Spirit/Gift society lies in the Transcendent – beyond the control of the Breakers.

10. Sustainability

Keepers practice economic inclusivity with both past and future generations. They call it "Seventh Generation" thinking. To take no action without considering the consequences of those actions upon the next seven generations.

Menders will revive this practice, not as a quaint ritual, but as prudent economic planning.

The purpose of governance
is to guide and shape the
behavior of each for the
good of all.

Each of us, every being on
this planet, has freedom,
volition and permission,
exercised in relationship to
all beings, within the Web of
Life. This is what it means
to be "empowered".

When all beings are freely
exercising freedom, volition
and permission, the Web
of Life is mutually self-
governing.

The Role of Power and Governance in the Relational Operating System

Breaker Power

Breaker Consciousness and its actors have destroyed, interrupted and violated the basic power relationships of freedom, volition and permission. Breakers have tried to enslave all beings; they have even enslaved themselves.

To Breakers, the purpose of governance is to amass power and control in the hands of a few. The basic expression of Breaker power is empire. Breaker Culture is steering us directly over a cliff. This is called "progress".

Mender Power

Menders acknowledge the natural, self-governing principles of the Web of Life. Menders will restore humans to their appropriate place within the Web of Life, and will heal the damages done by Breaker Consciousness.

3 Key Aspects of Relational Power

1. Emergence

Good governance naturally emerges when beings are in authentic proximity to each other, have common values, common rules and common visions. This is the key to Mender governance: authentic people in living systems naturally know what to do.

Politics is the art of looking for trouble, finding it whether it exists or not, diagnosing it incorrectly, and applying the wrong remedy.

Ernest Benn

Power doesn't corrupt people, people corrupt power.

William Gaddis

Any ideology that does not promote global understanding is failing the test of time.

Karen Armstrong

Mender politics will be based on "emergence" and "Emergent Systems". What is an "Emergent System"? Emergent systems are "complex adaptive systems that operate from low-level rules yet display high-level sophistication." Another way to see emergence is as a set of self-organizing principles.

The Orange Revolution in Kiev. The Rose Revolution in Georgia. The Cedar Revolution in Lebanon. The People's Movement in Nepal. And the famous Velvet Revolution in Czechoslovakia. These are all examples of emergent political power. In emergence, the will of the people is experienced as a direct, joyous, consensual, spontaneous outpouring of political energy. Acting without leaders or direction from above, these revolutions have acted to transform governments around the world. They have been successful where violent actions have failed.

The next phase for political emergence is to sustain the "people power" emergence past the presenting issues.

Emergent systems are leaderless in the traditional sense of a "leader" in control of the organization or system. (There is a role for a "leader" in an emergent system (see below), but not the "power-over" roles that we experience in Breaker Consciousness.)

There are five key characteristics of emergent political systems:

1. They have a <u>large number</u> of independent local participants, all sharing information.
2. There is a <u>lack of control</u> over any individual's behavior – people act, not because they are *compelled* but because they are *convinced.*
3. The participants share a <u>common set of simple values (or rules)</u>.
4. The participants share a common set of largely <u>interchangeable roles</u>.
5. The participants share the <u>same goals and objectives</u>.

With these five characteristics, very large numbers of individuals can act together in very complex ways to achieve amazing results. The <u>SYSTEM ITSELF</u> learns, grows, develops and adapts, even though the individuals themselves may not be (and generally cannot be) aware of the overall conditions of the system.

An "emergent" system:
when a collection of <u>individuals</u>
start to behave as a single <u>entity</u>.

Is there a role for "leadership" in an emergent system? What are the roles of the emergent leader? Yes, there is a role, but not the "power-over" relationships we typically associate with "leadership". The role of the emergent leader is to make sure emergence happens. They do this when they:
- Encourage/stimulate lots of participants (critical mass)
- Articulate simple, consistent rules

- o Articulate simple, deep values and goals
- o ~~Articulate simple, appropriate roles~~
- o Take no direct command or control

Emergence happens from the bottom up.

2. Relational democracy

Thomas Jefferson envisioned that "democracy" would be synonymous with "local". He felt that the best government was the one that people controlled directly. He advocated that the most significant political unit, the seat of the U.S. Government, should be the size of a voting precinct or ward.

In this scheme, every person would be a direct and active participant in government, not a passive bystander, or someone for whom "politics" means pulling a lever in a voting booth every four years or so. In a relational democracy, the exercise of power becomes "real": not just talking, but also deciding – and living with the consequences of those decisions.

The article... nearest my heart is the division of counties into wards. These will be **pure and elementary republics, the sum** *of which taken* **together composes the State,** *and will make of the whole a true democracy...*

Each ward would thus be a small republic within itself, and **every man in the State would thus become an acting member of the common government...**

Thomas Jefferson [emphasis mine]

This would be truly "bottom up" governance, where the most important decisions affecting a person's life would be made locally and consensually. This would be the essence of empowerment.

We can live in a democracy where we all relate to each other.

No standing armies. No Congress making distant decisions, answering to elites and lobbyists. No national taxes. No influential multinational corporations padding the pockets of near-permanent legislators. Had we heeded Jefferson, we would be living in a fundamentally different world. Though two centuries late, we can still get there.

Sortition: Solving the Problem of Voting

Once government gets large enough, direct, participatory democracy becomes unwieldy and ultimately impossible. The problem of representational "democracy" lies in the fairness (or lack thereof) of the system of selecting representatives. "Democratic" voting processes collect more than their fair share of demagogues, wackos, corruptibles, and people who place their own interests above that of "the people". Because the voting process is easily corrupted by elites for their own purposes, "government of the people" quickly turns into "government of the elites". This is true world-wide. Democracy in theory is a great idea. Democracy as practiced leaves a lot to be desired.

So, relational democracy would replace "voting" with "sortition". Sortition is selecting representatives by random selection. We trust this process when it is time to select 12 impartial citizens to sit on a jury. We can also trust this process to select the people who write our laws.

Anyone who has been called to jury duty has experienced a sortition process. As potential jurors, we are acting as entities of the State. We do it as a part of our "civic duty" as citizens. We sit in the jury pool, wait to see if our names get called, participate in the trial if called upon and respond to questions regarding our fitness and impartiality. We make the system work.

We know why we could not have an impartial judicial system if people "ran" for seats on a jury. ALL THOSE ARGUMENTS ARE ALSO TRUE FOR LEGISLATORS AND LEGISLATURES.

A sortition process would be "corruption-resistant", would prevent "career politicians", and would truly reflect the people of an area. Party affiliation becomes irrelevant. People would be called at random to serve on the legislature, serve a fixed term of office and then "retire" from public service (at least until their number comes up again).

3. Deep Democracy

The Magnet: For inclusive democracy to work, there must be a positive reason for potential adversaries to work together; something that draws people together and provides a positive incentive for them to resolve difficulties. For example: potential adversaries coming together to help each other harvest the other's crops. They may not LIKE each other, but the harvest serves as a "magnet' pulling them into a common activity.

Each of us is an active
AGENT for a type of
society. A few of us are
Keeper agents. Most of us
are Breaker agents.

We must learn to become
Mender agents.

SEED #6: THE RELATIONAL AGENTS

The Relational Operating System will be catalyzed by people who, through the simple act of living Mender lives, will help motivate and move those humans who wish to transition from Breaker models into the Mender models.

What is an Agent?

An agent is a person who, while working independently, operates on behalf of someone or something else.

Breaker Agents

Analogy: The young "anarchists" were sitting outside of a pizza place in the Hawthorne District of Portland. Huddled around a table, smoking cigarettes, talking about "smashing the System".

They were an integral part of the Breaker System.

They were active agents for the Breaker Operating System they claimed to want to "smash". Their choice to smoke Camel Filters (as opposed to smoking nothing, or growing and processing their own tobacco, or at least rolling their own cigarettes) reflects the independent nature of an agent. No one makes them smoke; no one forces their smoking choices on them. It is their conscious choosing (and their unconscious following-along) that made them Breaker agents.

Mender Agents

A different example: a family decides that the food they will eat will be, whenever possible, local and organic. They employ a variety of means: they join a "Community Supported Agriculture" group, grow some of their own food, look for local and organic in the supermarket, shop at farmers markets. They are Mender agents.

Each of their actions reinforces the Relational Operating System. Each decision is full of relationships. No one forces any of their actions. But, each of their actions as agents makes the Relational System stronger. By being willing to spend a little more to support their choice for local and organic food, they send a powerful signal – money is not the highest value – relationship is.

The Mender agents hold the model and practice authenticity and inclusivity in their dealings with others. They are in service to the Divine, to the Earth and to all beings.

Unconscious Agents

Right now, each one of us is an active supporter of the Breaker Operating System. Some of us are active, willing and enthusiastic participants. Some (most people reading this book) are reluctant, hesitant, inadvertent supports. Many, perhaps most, are simply unconscious agents.

One of the hallmarks of the Breaker Operating System is its pervasiveness. It is extremely difficult to extricate oneself from its operations. The person who buys a Prius still has to buy gasoline. The person who buys all local food may still bank with a multi-national bank. The person who works to end an onerous piece of legislation is still participating in the adversarial political system.

This is the reason many people throw up their hands and wail, "You can't fight City Hall!" The rationale: if you can't do everything, don't bother to do anything.

Evolving Past the Status Quo

Menders occupy a powerful middle ground between the paralysis of despair and the paralysis of self-congratulatory partial steps toward change. Menders know that the road ahead is long. Menders know that, given the state of matters right now, the most we are capable of may in fact be partial or incomplete measures. Menders know that our goal is to celebrate what we are doing right now, and to KEEP PUSHING THE ENVELOPE. Keep working to "Build the Cathedral".

Menders also know that, without an understanding of the comprehensive nature of the Breaker system, it is possible for potential Menders to get stuck in half measures. Half measures can look like a whole lot when one compares oneself to people who aren't changing at all. We all know people stuck in "I recycle, so I don't have to do anything else". It's time for all of us to get unstuck.

In the "Star Wars" movies, the Jedi Knights kept order in the Galaxy through their internal discipline, alignment with "The Force", moral persuasion... and the light saber.

We will accomplish the same thing... but without the necessity of high-tech weaponry.

The Breaker agents work within a toxic operating system. Changing the behavior of individuals does not change the operating system. We must change to a Mender Consciousness AND a Relational Operating System.

It's not enough to know that you are immersed in the Breaker society. You must know how you are going to get out, how you are going to shift your behavior from Breaker-centric to Mender-centric.

There are two futures facing the human family: the Breaker future and the Mender future.

Only one of these is viable.

SEED #7: NEXT STEPS FOR HUMANITY

Building the Cathedral – An Act of Faith

"We are entering a new land – some of us as intentional immigrants, most of us as refugees."

International Futures Forum

If we are going to fix this planet, we must first fix ourselves. If we are going to truly engage in healing, we Menders have to take a long view, see the bigger picture. The Relational Operating System starts a process that none of us alive today will see completed. I call this, "Building the Cathedral".

All of us have seen pictures of the grand Cathedrals of Europe. Building them took hundreds of years, in some cases over half a millennia, for their completion.

The cathedral designers thought long term. The designers envisioned a structure beyond the technological abilities of their time… an act of faith. The workers showing up to work was an act of faith. The very act of putting the wall up was an act of faith. They were working on a project that they did not start and would not finish. Their children's, children's, children's, children finished those walls.

Our task is to envision a societal shift that is so profound, yet so doable, that our lives and those of our descendants are taken up in the task. We have to replace our current multi-generational tasks called "making money and being entertained" with something more meaningful and more spiritually satisfying.

One of the key elements of my definition of spirituality is to be engaged in processes that go beyond the five senses. To recognize that LIFE is not confined to sensate experience. If I'm only thinking in terms of in my lifespan, if I'm only thinking of things that affect my physical comfort, then I'm not experiencing the kind of spirituality that can get us out of the Mess that we're in.

If I am truly in relationship with those on our planet who are not as fortunate as I am, if I'm concerned about those who haven't been born yet, if I take into consideration those on our planet who comprise the more-than-human world, then my actions are going to be spiritual actions.

A 1,000 Year Plan for Humanity

In a way, it is pure foolish speculation on my part to try to envision a 1,000 year plan. The likelihood that I'll get it wrong greatly outweighs the slim chance I'll get it right. But, there is value in making this vision, if it stimulates you to try to do better.

I think back to a science fiction book that I read, "Icehenge" by Kim Stanley Robinson, written in 1985. In the book, humans left Earth and were starting a voyage to the nearest star. At one point, the voyagers were busy loading their ship with paper books, boxes of music on audio tapes… The story was written before the advent of the modern computer. The author could not envision carrying hundreds of books and thousands of songs on a device that can fit on your keychain.

Similarly, WE cannot envision what lies beyond the next technological turn in the road. For the first time in human history, our technological abilities exceed our imagination. Ten years ago, we could not envision what the Internet can do today. Right now, we cannot envision what the Internet will be doing ten years from now.

This must change. Becoming Menders will free our imagination by harnessing our vision. By HAVING a vision, we become free and empowered beings. By making a 1,000 Year Plan, I free my imagination.

By envisioning our future, we direct and shape it. By envisioning a world filled with killer military nano-robots, that's what we'll experience. By envisioning a world with NO NEED FOR A VIOLENT MILITARY, our descendants get to live in THAT world. So, the only question is: which one do you want to give to your grandchildren and to the Earth?

So, regardless of how hilarious this may look to future generations (or even next year), here is my take on our 1,000 year plan.

Breaking the Shell:
Getting the Next 20 Years Right
If we don't get the next 20 years right, we

won't get a second chance. We won't have to worry about the next 1,000 years or even the next 100. We've got to get serious about our evolution.

An Exit/Entrance Strategy & Roadmap

Start living a post-petroleum lifestyle now and avoid the rush.

Richard Heinberg

It's not enough to recycle, buy local organic food and buy a Prius (or even ride a bike). That's the <u>beginning</u> of a process that completely extracts all beings on our planet from the Breaker mind-set.

You should think about your actions as falling into three different areas:

- **Status Quo Strategies:** Actions that support and maintain the Breaker Operating System. (Plan "A" thinking)
- **Transit Strategies:** Actions that help transit you out of the Breaker Operating System and help you to enter a Relational Operating System.
- **Mender Strategies:** Actions that support and maintain the Relational Operating System.

If you are not aware of your exit/entrance strategy, or you don't think one is necessary, by default, you are supporting the continuation of the Breaker system.

It is important not to think that your "Transit" strategies are true "Mender" strategies. Buying a Prius or other hybrid is a TRANSIT strategy. They still use fossil fuels and are single occupancy, single ownership vehicles. The Prius will <u>lead</u> to real solutions, and as such, should be welcomed as a transit strategy. But, if we act like they are the <u>solution</u>, they are a roadblock to finding real solutions.

How Do You Measure Success?

One of the most convenient – and insidious – aspects of Breaker Consciousness is its ability to reduce all values to one – money. A person with more money is judged as more successful than a person who has less. A society that is able to funnel more money up to already rich people (and/or funnels more power to State actors) is considered more successful than a society where everyone has enough and where everyone shares power.

But, how do you measure success with Mender Consciousness? For Menders, it is clear that money measures <u>something</u>, but it cannot measure or replace those things which have meaning for life – happiness, fulfillment, spiritual satisfaction.

For this, I have worked toward a "Happiness-Fulfillment/Misery Index". We can find the way to measure success by simply asking ourselves the right questions, and keeping track of the answers.

It is Time for Us to Let Go of "Normal"

At present, all of the policies of every government are based on a concept called "normal". The role of government is to maintain "normal", or to get us back to "normal" when we've left it, after the crisis has passed.

When "normal" means a reinvigoration of the Breaker Operating System, the system that caused the crisis in the first place, the faster we let go of "normal", the better off we all will be.

We are entering a phase where the Earth will heal Herself. She is going to come back into dynamic equilibrium. Whether or not we will be a part of that equilibrium greatly depends on our actions over the next 20 years.

There are no quick fixes.

In 100 Years: Dealing with the "Big 3": Food, Water and Energy

The three factors of food, water and energy are the key elements of the "Perfect Storm" that threatens to sweep humanity off of the planet.

Breaker approaches will exacerbate the problems. There will be no techno-fixes to these challenges. Technology follows consciousness, not the other way around. Breaker "solutions" will make things worse instead of better.

In a strange way, these three seemingly disparate matters all have the same simple solution: food, water and energy must become intensely local.

In the Breaker mind-set, food, water and energy all come from "somewhere else". All travel through pipelines or transportation networks thousands of miles in length. Each comes from one unstable region (from having too little) to a different kind of unstable region (from having too much). This system exists for one reason: monetary profit. It is the ONLY way that the system makes conceptual sense.

In the Mender mind-set, each region, each eco-system, will be responsible for its own food, water and energy. Growers in the Amazon basin will not be tempted to cut down the trees to plant soybeans – there will be no global market that turns soybeans into dollars. Every region, every city, every building will grow or absorb its own energy needs – there will be no global energy markets that destabilize entire regions in a mad dash to pump out the last dregs of fossil fuels.

Modern society has relieved us of the burden of growing, harvesting, even preparing our daily bread, in exchange for the burden of simply paying for it.

National Geographic, 6/2009 issue

In a Mender economy, economic power grows out of the ground, or falls from the sky, or radiates from the Sun. It doesn't have to be controlled and doesn't need to be hoarded.

With Mender Consciousness, we will all see that food, water and energy are all sacred Gifts from the Divine, and should be held with the awe, reverence and respect that they deserve. 100 years from now, the idea of buying, selling or making a profit off of food or water or energy will be as morally repugnant as slavery.

In 100 Years: The End of Violence

Violence in the Breaker Operating System is endemic. The Breaker societies are BUILT on a foundation of violence as a means to gain power and maintain control.

Violence is ubiquitous, popular and out of control. Right now, there are 100 wars raging on our planet. The U.S. government spends MOST of its wealth on violence, hundreds of billions of dollars every year – no questions asked.

All of this is based on the Breaker concept of separation – that security is based on separation and control, rather than inclusivity and engagement.

Putting a Bell – And a Harness – on the Cat

A large military, such as the U.S. military, does have a use, once it is oriented away from violence and killing. It's easier (and much cheaper) to win friends than to try to control enemies. Menders discover that "we" will be more secure when "they" also feel secure.

You remember the children's story about the mice that band together to sneak up on the house cat and hang a bell from its neck, so they can tell when the cat is on the prowl. We need to do more; we need to put a work harness on this particular cat, to have our military and the world's militaries ready, trained, equipped and anxious to be deployed to solve some of our most intractable problems.

By reorienting the world's militaries away from violence, incredible creativity and human energy can be released and realized. We know that the oceans will rise and that a billion people will need to be relocated into new cities. No problem. We know that food and water will need to be distributed to hundreds of millions. No problem. We know that the possibility for many more New Orleans type disasters awaits our planet. No problem...

With a huge military and a huge budget for compassionate assistance instead of killing, these challenges (and many others) can be resolved, with compassion and creativity.

Just imagine how we can face and respond to our pending disasters, spending hundreds of billions of dollars a year on restoration, recovery, and world-wide development – no questions asked.

In 500 Years: Terraforming Earth

I think the scientists and explorers are right: there is something in us that makes us want to learn, to explore, to search out new frontiers. There's nothing wrong with that.

But, we don't get to do that exploration while the human family suffers. We don't get to carry our Breaker consciousness to other planets.

When things evolve, they get more beautiful.

Ray Kurzweil

Right now, there are six scientists whizzing over our heads on the International Space Station. It costs billions to keep them there. They look down on one billion humans who could live for a year on what it costs to keep six people overhead for a day.

The space station is not a bad idea... it IS a bad priority. Human beings should have a different set of priorities. Human beings should put humans first, life first, Earth first.

The Breaker mindset reverses human priorities. When money comes first, life comes last.

In 500 years, Menders will be actively engaged in changing the face of the Earth. Gently, respectfully, and working with all aspects of the Web of Life, Menders will work to increase the life force on this planet. That means reducing the size of the deserts, increasing the amount of fresh water on the planet, living in dynamic equilibrium with all other living beings.

Right now, a large percentage of the Earth's surface already resembles Mars – lifeless, barren terrain. Instead of going all the way to Mars to make that planet look like a model of Earth, we should stop trashing this one and start treating it with respect. We can gradually, respectfully and reverently green the surface of our own planet.

In 1,000 Years: Terraforming Mars

For those of us who think in cycles, a thousand years isn't that long. If we have a plan that transcends "money", we will give purpose to our lives and a positive legacy to our descendants.

Yes, let's expand Life beyond this particular planet. Let's be an active part of the spread of Life in the Universe, by spreading Life to our nearest neighbors – Venus and (more likely) Mars.

BUT… we don't get to go outside to play until we clean our room first. (How many of us heard that from our mothers?) Breaker exploration has always been "Let's find another place to trash."

Let's terraform Mars, but not the way we have changed the environment of Earth. Let's not spread the Breaker biocidal consciousness one step further.

I have been in thousand-year-old olive groves in Palestine and marveled at the husbandry that was required to keep those up. Fifty generations and nary one grandson failed to carry the water up to the grove in dry months in all that time.

Albert Bates

AFTERWORD:

Now, you've just been given a handful of seeds. How do you turn that into an apple orchard or a field of wheat?

A seed is a promise. It's a tiny packet of energy. If you add sunlight, soil and water, that seed will bring forth a miracle. I want to repeat Thoreau's quote here:

> *Though I do not believe that a plant will spring up where no seed has been, I have great faith in a seed. Convince me that you have a seed there, and I am prepared to expect wonders.*

- Henry David Thoreau

If you take your handful of seeds and put them on your bookshelf, I'm pretty sure nothing will happen.

So… where will you plant the seeds contained in this book? With whom will you share your seeds? How?

If you are waiting for a book with complete answers, this is not it. Nor will "Spirit on Earth" be such a book. There cannot be a book or a person or a group with all the "right" answers, who have the total plan.

You will never find it, if you are looking outside of yourself. YOU are the seed.

Look at what a seed does. The secret is sealed inside, the potential hidden. Inside, it is only potential. It must break open, stretch out, gain energy by being IN its environment, not sealed off from it.

So must you. Both our challenges and this book provide you an opportunity to break open, to express your gifts, to live your potential, to get fed, to feed others.

This is time of transformation. A butterfly is NOT a caterpillar with wings stuck on. (That would never get off of the ground.) In order for the butterfly to emerge, it must COMPLETELY CONSUME the caterpillar. It must transform every trace of caterpillar-ness.

We are inside humanity's chrysalis. All of our actions, one way or another, will lead to our transformation. For those of us who share this consciousness, this is a remarkable and rewarding journey, a true adventure. If not, this may seem like the "end of the world". The events will be the same... the only difference is whether we are participants or spectators.

This is not "my" journey. It's not "yours", either. It's ours....

You are the seed. I am prepared to expect wonders.